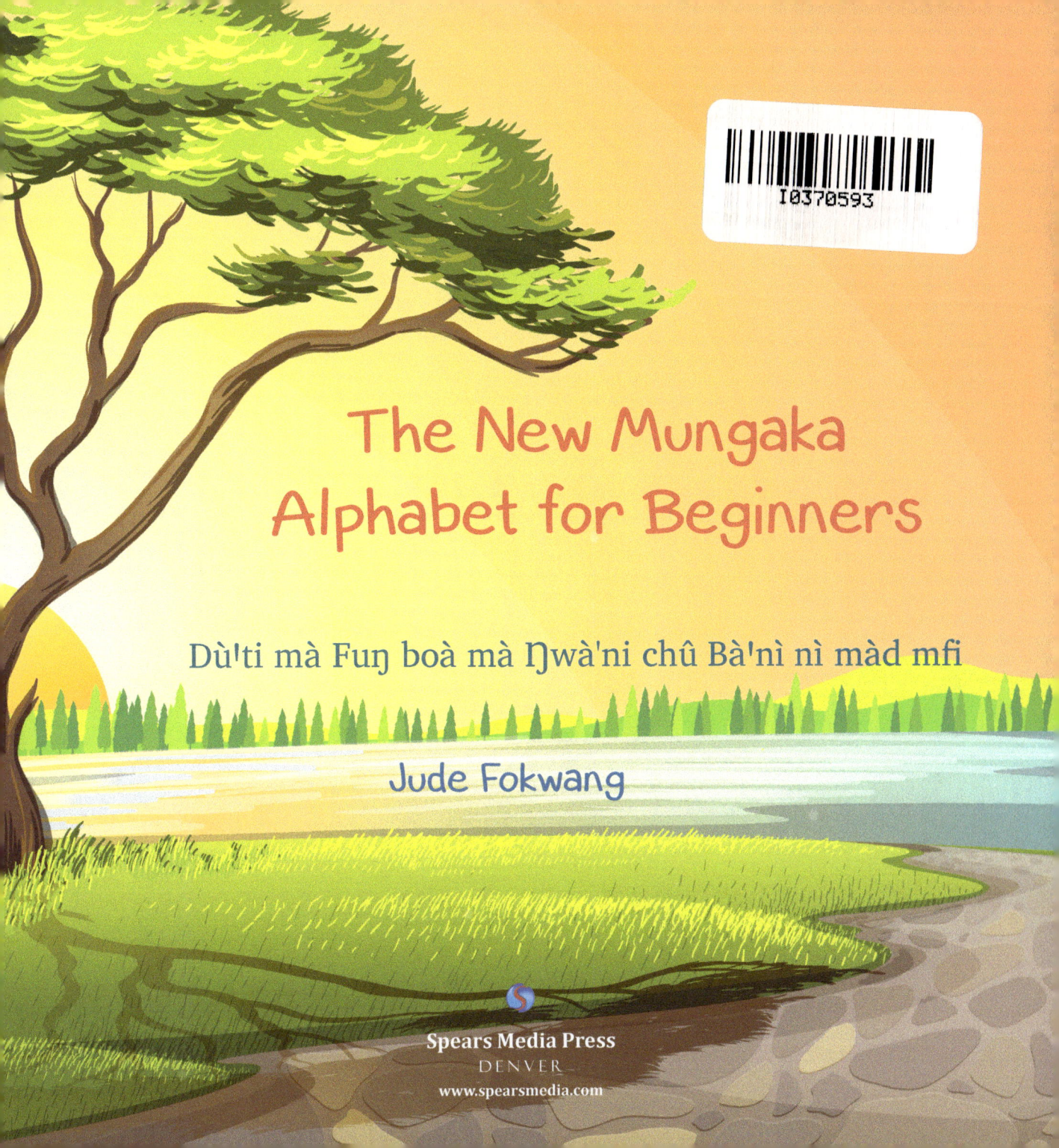

The New Mungaka Alphabet for Beginners

Dùˈti mà Fuŋ boà mà Ŋwàˈni chû Bàˈnì nì màd mfi

Jude Fokwang

Spears Media Press
DENVER
www.spearsmedia.com

Spears Media Press LLC
DENVER
7830 W. Alameda Ave, Suite 103-247 Denver, CO 80226
United States of America

First Published in 2017 by Spears Media Press
www.spearsmedia.com
info@spearsmedia.com
Information on this title: www.spearsmedia.com/product/Mungaka-Alphabet
© 2017 Jude Fokwang
All rights reserved.

No part of this publication may be reproduced, distributed, or transmitted in any form or by any means, including photocopying, recording, or other electronic or mechanical methods, without the prior written permission of the publisher, except in the case of brief quotations embodied in critical reviews and certain other noncommercial uses permitted by copyright law. For permission requests, write to the publisher, addressed "Attention: Permissions Coordinator," at the address above.

Ordering Information:
Special discounts are available on bulk purchases by corporations, associations, and others. For details, contact the publisher at any of the addresses above.

ISBN: 9781942876205 (Paperback)

Spears Media Press has no responsibility for the persistence or accuracy of urls for external or third-party internet websites referred to in this publication, and does not guarantee that any content on such websites is, or will remain, accurate or appropriate.

Spring 2019 Edition - corrected for tones and spelling.

For Ma Andin, my first Mungaka tutor
&
Kǎ Lydia, our matriarch

Dear Reader,

Mungaka is a language of over 500,000 native speakers world wide. It is the principal language of more than 120,000 citizens resident in the town of Bali Nyonga in northwestern Cameroon. Mungaka emerged in the mid-1800s and became a popular medium for education and trade when German explorers colonized the region in the late 1890s. Following German colonization the Basel Mission adopted Mungaka as the language of literacy and liturgy in its schools and churches respectively until the mid 20th century. Today, Mungaka remains a popular language in Christian music and the preferred medium of communication among Bali Nyonga citizens and their kith and kin in the diaspora.

While native speakers refer to the language as Chu Bà'nì (that is, the Bali language), linguists simply refer to it as Mungaka (Mìŋgâkà). The name Mungaka is composed of three syllables; **Mì** - [I], **ŋgâ**- [say], **kà** - (an emphatic particle). This reader aims to complement the fantastic job being done in Bali Nyonga by the Mungaka Rehabilitation Committee (MRC) since 2010. The MRC is the leading trainer of teachers and pupils in the reading and writing of Mungaka.

Although Mungaka has existed in written form for over a century, most native speakers hardly wrote the language due to the lack of proper training in the "old" Mungaka alphabet. The creation of the MRC in 2010 was primarily aimed at revitalizing and accelerating the pace of Mungaka's use as a written language. The timing couldn't be better. Today, we are blessed with access to smartphones and portable computers, tools that will greatly facilitate the writing of Mungaka based on the new standardized alphabet.

When you learn to read and write Mungaka, you will be joining a growing number of enthusiastic learners the world over, who aspire to be part of those magical social moments when native speakers share jokes, tell stories and pass on time-honored witty sayings. Needless to add that by learning Mungaka, you will develop a deeper appreciation for Bali culture.

The basis of learning to read and write any language is in mastering its alphabet. This short colorful book contains 29 individual or combined letters that will help you learn to read and write Mungaka. As Mungaka is a tonal language, you will also learn to distinguish between different tones which tend to change the meaning of words depending on how they are pronounced. The tones can be distinguished by four different symbols which, when combined, amount to 33 symbols/sounds in the modern Mungaka alphabet.

Each letter or combination of letters are illustrated with photos of objects or actions that best represent the speech sounds. A companion Kindle Edition enhanced with sound is also available to accelerate your mastery of the pronunciation of the letters or speech sounds.

I hope you enjoy learning the new Mungaka alphabet and that before long, you'll be showing off your new skill to friends and family.

— Jude Fokwang

The Mungaka Alphabet

Below is a list of the standard Mungaka alphabet or sound system. These letters or combinations are also known as *graphemes* which mean they are the smallest meaningful contrastive unit in a writing system.

Grapheme Uppercase	Grapheme Lowercase	Grapheme Uppercase	Grapheme Lowercase
A	a	K	k
B	b	L	l
CH	ch	M	m
D	d	N	n
E	e	Ny	ny
Ɛ	ɛ	Ŋ	ŋ
Ə	ə	O	o
F	f	Ɔ	ɔ
G	g	P	p
GH	gh	S	s
H	h	T	t
I	i	U	u
Ɨ	ɨ	V	v
J	j	W	w
		Y	y

Tones in Mungaka

Mungaka, like many African languages is tonal. This means that words spelled in a similar fashion may have different meanings depending on how they are pronounced. Four main tones will be distinguished as seen in the table below.

	Diacritic	Graph or symbol	Examples
1	Low level (LL)	`	Bàm (bag) Màli – beans Tàŋ – ceiling Tà – insect, father of
2	High level (HL)	´	Taŋ – math, count Ta – play, sew
3	Falling	^	Mômbɔd – baby Mâŋgɔb - Mother hen
4	Rising	ˇ	Fŭb – sip a hot drink Fĕd – blow Lă - pass by Lăb, flog, beat

Glottal Stop: ꞌ

Examples: Vəꞌti, (extinguish) Tǎꞌ (search) bɔ̌ꞌ (mushroom).

A glottal stop is a speech sound produced by closing the vocal cords and then opening them quickly so that the air from the lungs is released with force. In some anglicized spellings, words that ought to have a glottal stop are often spelled with an "h".

How to Type the New Alphabet on Your Computer

You won't need to purchase a new keyboard in order to type the new Mungaka alphabet on your computer. For a start, you will need to download two free applications available for both Mac OS and Windows PCs: **Keyman Desktop 9.0** available at: https://keyman.com/desktop/ and the **Cameroon Keyboard** available at: http://keymankeyboards.com/?q=Cameroon

This keyboard supports all Cameroon languages with a single, standardized layout based on the US English keyboard. Choose the Unicode version and click download. A layout of the keyboard is provided below for your convenience.

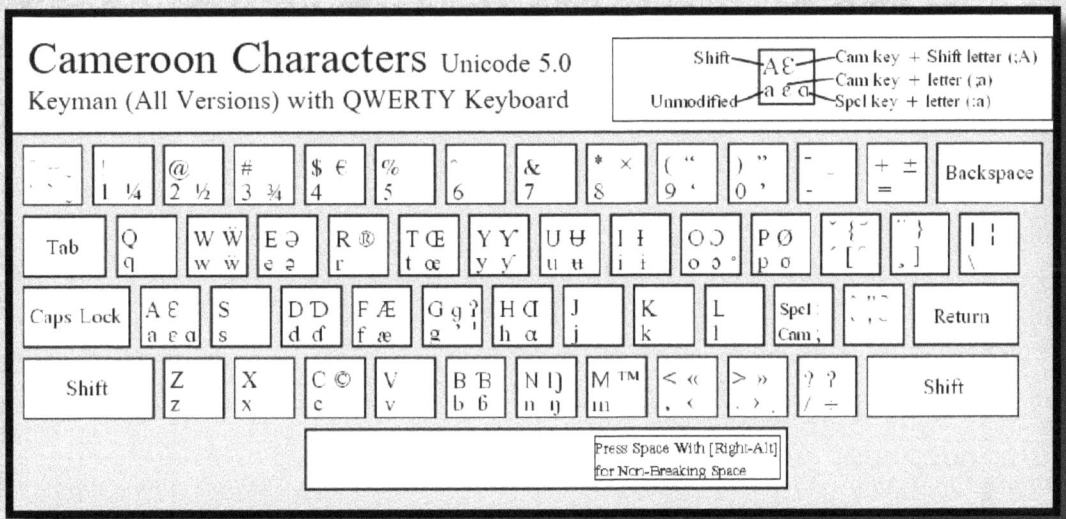

Once you have downloaded both applications, first install the Keyman Desktop, followed by the Cameroon keyboard which you can easily install from within the Keyman Desktop application. One final task is to install suitable font types that would display the alphabet correctly. Download and install any of the following fonts: **Charis SIL** or **Doulos SIL** and you're ready to start typing. The **Cambria** font which comes installed in most computers is also equiped to render the Mungaka alphabet.

How do you type the appropriate keyboard combinations to get the right alphabet? Follow the same link to download the Cameroon keyboard and click on the link titled "view documentation". Download and print out the document for easy reference when typing on your keyboard. A downscaled table of the combinations is provided overleaf for your convenience.

Character	Type	Code	Character	Type	Code		Diacritic	Graph	Type
ɑ	:a	0251	ɑ̄	;H	F208		low	ˋ	'
ɛ	;a	025B	ɨ	;i	0268		high	ˊ	[
Ɛ	;A	0190	Ɨ	;I	0197		falling	ˆ	"
ɓ	;b	0253	ŋ	;n	014B		rising	ˇ	{
Ɓ	;B	0181	Ŋ	;N	014A		nasal	ˎ	]
ɗ	;d	0257	ɔ	;o	0254		tilde	~	~
Ɗ	;D	018A	Ɔ	;O	0186		mid	-	-
ə	;e	0259	ø	;p	00F8		dieresis	¨	}
Ə	;E	018F	Ø	;P	00D8		vert. mid	'	ˋ
æ	;f	00E6	œ	;t	0153		high-mid	ˊ	:[
Æ	;F	00C6	Œ	;T	0152		low-mid	ˋ	:'
ǀ	:g	02C8	ʉ	;u	0289		mid-high	ˇ	:{
ʼ	;g	02BC	Ʉ	;U	0244		mid-low	ˋ	:"
ʔ	:G	0294	ẅ	;w	1E85		tilde und	~	:~
ɡ	;G	0261	ƴ	;y	01B4		dot under	.	:.
α	;h	03B1	Ƴ	;Y	01B3				

I'd suggest that you have a print out of the Cameroon Characters Keyboard, positioned in an area where you may easily cross-check the combinations as you type. The first couple of attempts may seem challenging but as you practice more, you will become efficient in typing the key combinations. Practice, they say, makes perfect. Happy reading and writing the new Mungaka alphabet.

Aa

Tab – shoes

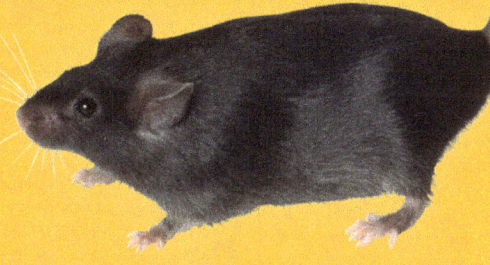
Mbàb - mouse

Bàm – bag

Ndab - house

Bb

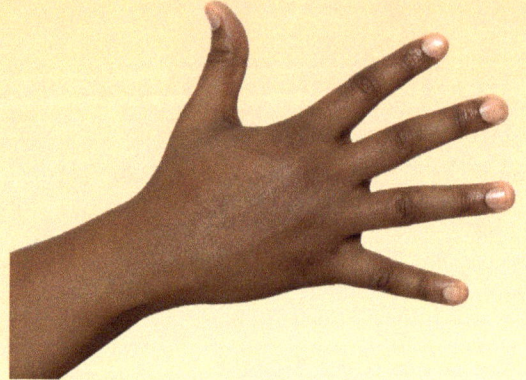
Bo – hand/arm

Bon – children

Botɨ – branch

CHch

Chinji – soap

chə̌'tu - hat

Chi – Salt

Chìchwè – hairy caterpillar

Dd

Dù – honey, bee

Dùma – shirt/singlet

Dàŋdàŋ - arm-drum

Ee

Kěˈfɨn – key

Kè - mat

Nswen - Elephant

Ɛɛ

Kɛ̌d - pour off/Spill

Bɛn - dance

Fɛdfɛd – brothers/sisters/siblings

Njə̀mbi - sheep

Lə̀ŋ – chair

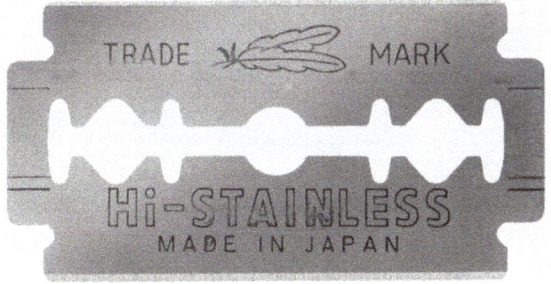

Kə̀m – razor

Ff

Fed – press

Fǎ! - work

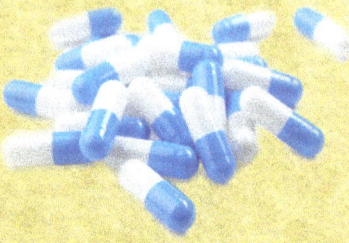

Fù – medicine

Fò – chief/king

Gg

Ga – bamboo flute

Gwǎnyìnyi - hyena

Gàri – cassava flour

GHgh

Ghɨgha – butterfly

Ghan – thief

Ghɨghàŋ - okra

Ghàbti – share

Hh

Hĕ - exclamation of astonishment

Hannah – female name

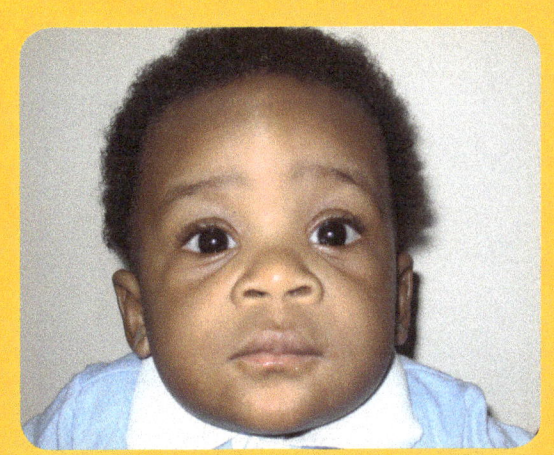

Henry – male name

Ii

2
Iba – two

3
Ited – three

5
Itàn - five

4
Ikwà – four

Ii

Kĭm – nail something

Misiŋ – bird

Kĭb – crack

Jj

Jam – bear fruit

Jə'tì – broom

Ja'ni – dry

Kk

Kùŋndìm - owl

Kimàŋkɔ̀' - tortoise

Kwăkùd - parrot

Ll

Ləm – bat

Lilì - mosquito

Lam – marry

Mm

Mândìkàŋ - umbrella

Mǎlàm – mirror

Mànjì – road

Nn

Nsu - fish

Naŋ – cook

Nji – dress

Njinjì - fly

Nyny

Nyo – snake

Nyŏmnyôm – worm

Nyàmbà'nì – horse

Nyùm - sun

Ŋ ŋ

ŋgab – antelope

ŋgàn – crocodile

ŋgɔb – hen, chicken

ŋgɛ̀n – grasshopper

Oo

So – hoe

Sòŋkù – trouser/pants

Sogè - soldier

Bom – mold, form

Ɔɔ

Ŋkɔ̂ŋfɨn – wasp

Bɔ̀ꞌ - mushroom

Mbɔꞌ - groundnut/ peanut pudding

Mbɔ̀ꞌmbàb – guinea pig

Pp

Pàdŋkwèn – knapsack/rug sack

Pepà - paper

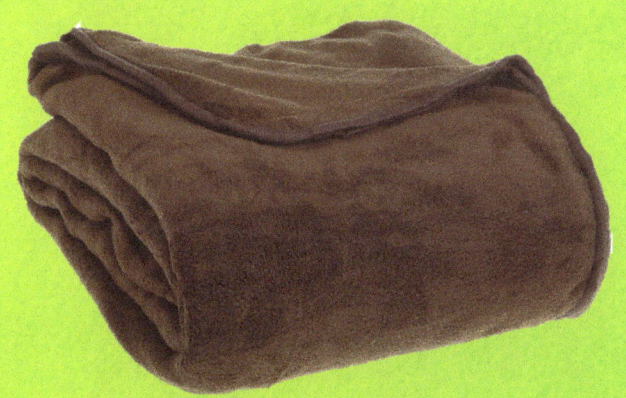

Plàŋkɨtɨ - blanket

Ss

Swìbo - nine

Sàd – comb

Sisi – black/brown

Saꞌnsi – well, spring

Tt

Tìtɔ̀ⵏ - toad

Tàmnsòn – frog

Tăchì – cricket

Uu

Ch**u** – speak, talk

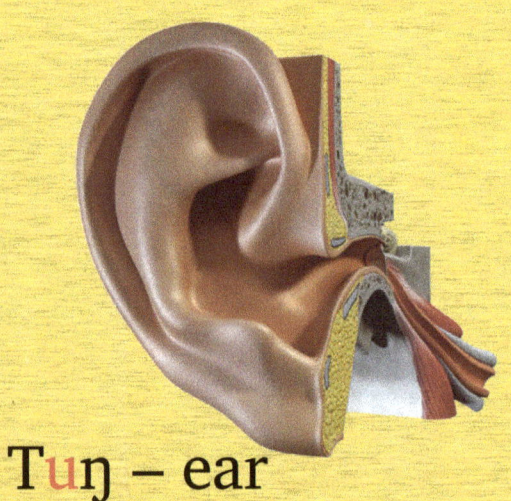

T**u**ŋ – ear

Ch**u**' - taro porridge

Vv

Vəˈti – extinguish, put out

Vàvà – nchǐ vàvà – waterfall

Vum (vɨm) – hunting

Ww

Wo - stone

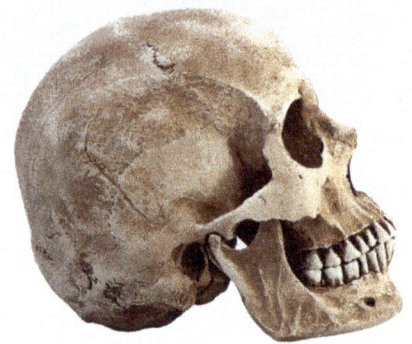

Wɔlɔˈtu - skull

Wɔ̀btì – ring

Wɔm – ten

Yy

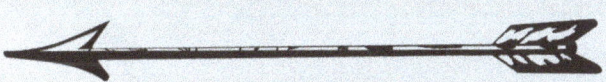

Yolì – arrow

Yumtası̀' – toy, plaything

Yeba – female name

BODY PARTS IN MUNGAKA

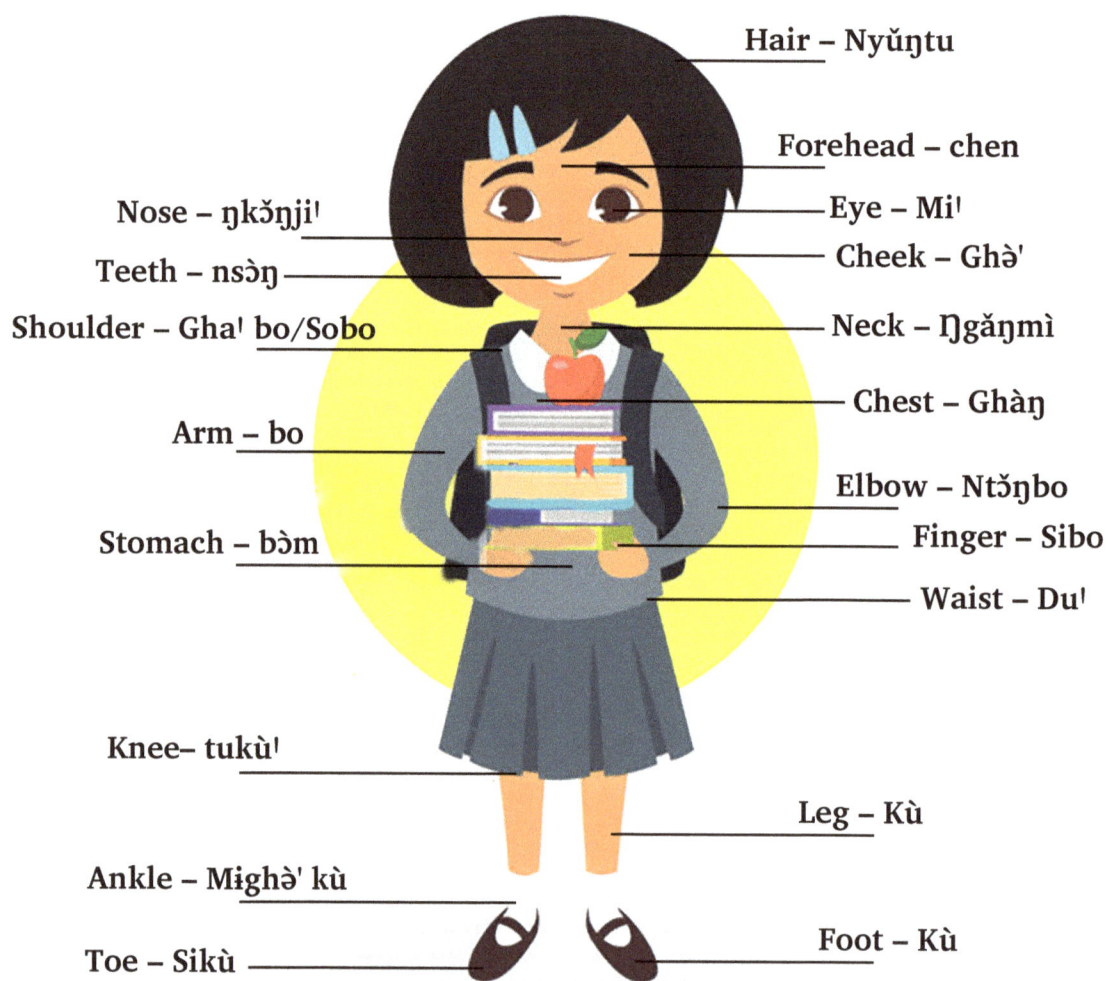

www.ingramcontent.com/pod-product-compliance
Lightning Source LLC
Chambersburg PA
CBHW051249110526
44588CB00025B/2933